The author has a background in the health profession. Writing has been a passion right from a young age but much of it has been in the world of health sciences. Amateur poetry and fiction writing started in the early years of secondary education but became a background activity during the years of higher education and career progression.

Other interests include playing the acoustic guitar, travelling and watercolour painting.

To the love of my life, Evv

Bessie Barbara Badge

LOVE, THE MOON AND THE STARS

AUSTIN MACAULEY PUBLISHERS™

LONDON · CAMBRIDGE · NEW YORK · SHARJAH

A CIP catalogue record for this title is available from the British Library.

ISBN 9781528916172 (Paperback)
ISBN 9781528961479 (ePub e-book)

www.austinmacauley.com

First Published (2019)
Austin Macauley Publishers Ltd
25 Canada Square
Canary Wharf
London
E14 5LQ

I would like to thank my family for their enthusiastic encouragement.

The Moment

I turned to say goodbye and looked
At your beautiful eyes that were full
Of love, life from me, had snooked.
I couldn't resist the pull.

Our eyes locked and moistened.
Our lips parted and smiled into our eyes.
Our voices caressed each other and softened
As we sent each other into love's highs.

A strong magnetic force thrust
At me. I fought to stay still
Merge into you I must
Resistance worn beyond will.

My lips found their way
To yours. I still tried hard to resist
Love beginning to hold sway
Germinating in our hearts to exist.

Ah, just at the last minute
I forced my lips to your cheek
Strong willed, yet with a force so minute.
Into your heart I took a peek.

You furtively smiled as you sought
Deep into my soul and found
Love that no longer fought
But gave you a glow so profound.

I smiled as I beheld you glowing
Radiant throughout your body.
I felt contented within, knowing
Our hearts sang love's rhapsody.

Wordsmith

You do fashion a word
Yet don't know you are a wordsmith
With a double edged sword
You forge a heart to the pith.

Words plain and simple
My heart they conduct.
Chords that can't be played in single
Till a tear is shed from a duct.

You could be silent, yet speak.
With the hammer of words
Shape me to the peak
Of the heart's orchestral chords.

With innocence, you
Sing me to my slaughter
Like the proverbial ewe
Till death I accept with laughter.

The wordsmith of my core
My web, spins to an encore
The chorus of words said before
And memories washed ashore.

The Caress of Your Words

The caress of your words
Gentle and sharp
Like tips of swords
And notes of a harp.

To a crescendo
My heart strings you play.
With innuendo
You say.

"I trust you,"
You say.
Resist you?
If I may.

"Stay…"
You start to say
And play
My heart's violin, your way.

My heart I lay
'Tween the twin peaks
Dare I say
Of your breast, me speaks.

My emotions you undress
With eyes that caress.
Of life's woes, I care less.
Your words, they caress.

The First Time

The first time I
Beheld you, my
I refused to accept I
Was bowled over, why.

Subtle to the heart were
Cupid's arrows there
From your beauty, where
Could I escape, if anywhere.

Overpowered without a fight
Saw I the light.
A love so right
Lit up the night.

Dressed simple with no frill
With love's scent to fill
Silently to kill
A heart over a hill.

Like a gentle breeze of chloroform
The first time I awakened to your form
Dreams of love a norm
To love's sleep I conform.

The first time I cannot forget
Love holds no regret.
The sweet realisation, yet
Of the dawn of love's sunset.

The first time felt like the end
For our goodbyes to mend
What distance was to rend
Hearts apart, to send.

My Lovecin

You are the medicine called Lovecin
That fills my brain with oxytocin
Makes me sweet in every way
Causes my body and soul to sway
In your loving arms, I stay
My head over your beating heart, I lay.

The love hormone infused
Hearts and minds fused
Everything I view a beautiful landscape
Your love over my heart, a cape
Reaching beyond the nape
From which there is no escape.

Were my heart weak I would need digoxin.
But your love is no toxin.
Multi-layered like a leek
Quietly confident, yet meek
Your moves so sleek
As my heart to conquer, you seek.

How could I have refused?
With love to be confused
When you submerge me in love's pond
Transport me to heaven and beyond
As with the language of love we correspond
And my eyes and lips yield and respond.

My Lovecin
For which there is no penicillin.
A venom with no antidote.
Told only in an anecdote.
Life may have lent a lepidote.
That you beautify with epidote.

How Did You Find the Way to My Heart?

It was stone walled preserved.
Only for one person, so I
Told myself, my heart was fully served
Before you, now it's a lie.

All the bolts and nuts tight
I felt safe in my comfort zone
My heart a shadow with no light
Beating with a monotone.

Then, you came.
And shattered the stone
Wall, my heart to tame
And for lost time to atone.

Gentle wind that gathered.
Now a tropical cyclone.
Not that it mattered
How you were my brain's clone.

How did you find the way
To my heart and course through
the arteries and veins, anyway
For my love that you drew.

With such stealth and surprise
My defences you broke down
From the ruins, love to arise
With the unsettled dust to make a clown.

A Hundred Years

I stared at the moon
And thought
In the high tide of noon
A hundred years are like nought.

For you render
Time, vacuous and meaningless
Dull my senses with the lavender
Of love timeless and endless.

I can sit with you under
Stars that shine without caution
Hold you in the lightning and thunder
And wither the storm of our emotion.

A hundred years and over
I can listen to you endlessly
And know it can never be over
When hearts love relentlessly.

With you I can love
Put my head on the block
A hundred years and above
Forget time and its clock.

I could be tossed by the waves of life
And stay still by your side.
I could have my heart stabbed by a knife
Yet a hundred years, love and abide.

For a day in your presence
Is a hundred years times ten.
Our love's effervescence
Fragile like eggs of a hen.

Earthquake of Love

Side by side, hand in hand
Hearts tied by a band
Love full of clout
As we aimlessly walked about.

Then you turned
And your eyes burned.
My tears welled up to quench the fire
Lit by your heart's desire.

Our arms sought each
Other as we reach
The yearning itch so sore
Of love searing to the core.

The lips touched, it was no fun.
For the earth spun and spun
Moving below and above
In the earthquake of love.

Time stood still.
The earth moved at will
Yet we stayed standing
And that surpassed understanding.

The earth spun in the quake
Of love, we did not wake
Up the peaceful haze
Our kiss never to faze.

I clung to you as the ground
Beneath our feet spun around
As if dizzy with the fruit of the vine
In the quake of love divine.

Will Our Love Be the Greatest Love Story Ever Told?

When generations these pages hold
Will our love be told
As the greatest love story to behold
When the years unfold?

Will our love story provoke
The profound feelings we evoke
And fond memories that invoke
Time never to revoke?

As forever in my arms I hold
And keep your heart free from cold
Love you till we grow old
And years into one fold.

Will our love story be the greatest
To resist time and its test
Remain current and latest
And to light up hearts, be the fastest?

Will our love be the mold
That markets have never sold
And the young and the old
Earnestly desire to hold?

When a fire is lit or a lamp
For lovers out to camp
Will our love leave its stamp
And keep their hearts free from damp?

Will our love story be gilded in gold
So over the years as the pages unfold
It never ceases to amaze those who behold
The greatest love story ever told?

I Breathe and Feel You in the Breeze

In your absence
I feel your presence.
In my heart you ever live
A special love always to give.

I breathe and feel
You in the breeze like steel
Real, solid and firm
Tender whispers of love to affirm.

Light as wind, you gently caress.
Against my face, you press.
Your freshness, I take in
And feel my head spin.

I have surrendered to your charm
For you mean me no harm
In your arm, I lie
So we see, love, eye to eye.

You are the air I breathe and
From where I stand
I would shrivel and wilt away
Were you pray, from my life to stay.

I feel you and breathe you
Like air fresh and new.
Though far, you abound
In me and everywhere around.

Angel by the Doorway

There you stood.
Your eyes languidly focused
On me, I barely understood
The narrative being discussed.

Angel by the doorway
Adorned with such beauty
Held my gaze without sway
Your look demanded, it was my duty.

It was like a dream
Lit by the light colours of your dress
And the concealed smile you beam.
I was captivated I confess.

It was like heaven was beckoning
With your outstretched arms
Here was my time of reckoning
If I resist your charms.

There was no grace.
Your spell filled me with a high.
I fell into your embrace
Then your hug sent me to the sky.

To the Moon and the Stars

Love lifts a heart to defy
Gravity, so it can fly
Far to the planet mars
And to the moon and the stars.

When a heart is set free
It finds the energy to flee
From mortal things
As love gives it wings.

Our silhouette is a highlight
Of lovers in the moonlight
Oblivious of night and day
In each other's arms to stay.

Free from the confines
Of life's laws and fines
Love makes lovers transcend
To the stars they ascend.

To the moon and the stars
Hearts healed from scars
Won't let go of the chance
To love's tune, leap and dance.

Beyond the clouds and azure
It's all crystal clear and sure.
Love navigates through what mars
Our flight to the moon and the stars.

To the moon and the stars
Our hearts' stanzas and bars
A rhythm and rhyme brings
As the celestial, our love sings.

When You Look at the Stars

Are they just flickering
Lights for thoughts wandering
And fumbling in the dark
To find a place, for their souls to park?

When you look at the stars.
Do you see space cars
Bringing, my heart to you anew
With love you never knew.

Do they twinkle in my eyes
Cross the T's and dot the I's
And light up the fire
Of your heart's desire?

When you look at the stars.
Do you hear the notes of guitars
Plucking feelings that are profound
And know your heart, a home has found.

Do they shine bright
Show you the path that's right
Lead you to my loving arms
From wars full of wounding arms?

When you look at the stars.
Does your heart rise like notes of sitars?
To reach the celestial my love gives
And know how eternal and special our love lives.

When You Look at Me like That

I could go and fetch you gold
Many light years away
Even when we grow old
And winds our frail bodies sway.

When you look at me like that
You rocket me to Pluto and beyond
Not an eyelid would I bat
To your command I respond.

More and more to you
I want to give and give.
For each day that's new
I desire that you live and live.

For I don't want it to end
The way you look at me and
Touch deep inside to mend
My heart's ache with your hand.

When you look at me like that
The world becomes peaceful with no spat.
My heart feels your eyes' gentle pat
As our minds continue their chat.

The Glow on Your Face

The glow on your face
Was enough to melt
My heart and make it race
With feelings never before, felt.

Such beauty oozed, from inside
Out, your skin to set alight
Like an angel by the seaside
In the bright morning light.

Your happiness made you glow
My heart, with warmth, to awaken
And thoughts of love to sow
My heart from then on you had taken.

To your glow, my frozen heart thawed
Yet I stilled it, but not my lips
More and more, love, my heart gnawed
Our eyes, each other, peered for clues and tips.

I just had to give you that kiss.
Though I had not wanted to
My brain thinking it amiss
That my heart easily wanted to.

The glow on your face
A treasure in my heart, I hold.
It gives me strength to face
The trials of life and now I'm bold.

Into Your Arms

Into your arms
To run
Heart and mind in arms
The longing, no fun.

To die
In your arms
A lie
Your arms
To defy.

Thought love
'D be my death
As love
You showed its depth.

Yet I'm no dove
The peace of death
To love
My very breath
In your glove.

Into the rain
A heart without rest
The storm and pain
Of an emotional tempest.

In your arms
To die
Your charms
I defy
Yet crave 'ur arms.

Deep and Still

Where the river curves
It lies low
Like your curves.
An x-bow.

Deep and still
Looking cool
No frill, no shrill.
Still deep pool.

You hold me deep
And still
My heart you keep
With warmth to fill.

I shake with passion
Of a fashion
With no compassion
Just deep and still passion.

No Need for Words

Where true love
Soars like an eagle in
A seamless flight above
Words do not come in.

No need
For words that mar
Your perfect heart I heed
From distances afar.

When into your eyes
I pear
There are no lies.
Nor fear.

Step by step with
Strides that match
A rhythm and width
Only stars can watch

How can we part?
Your eyes say.
A feeble attempt to depart
Yet dazed I stay.

Hands reaching
Out from your eyes, hold
Me beseeching.
No need for words, be bold.

You watch me go, bemused
Heart calling, "No!"
In silence, confused
Eyes wrapping me, I can't go.

Through Rose-Tinted Glasses

There can only be one of you
Even if the world were made anew.
You are special and irreplaceable
Sweet memories of you, ineffaceable.

I know I saw you through
Rose tinted glasses that threw
My heart into a tailspin.
Now you are in my head like a hairpin.

I have painted you handsome.
On my canvas, wholesome
With muscles that a punch pack
And a stomach adorned with a six-pack.

My tinted vision gives you wings
Like Cupid, as he flies and sings
With your shining sword and glamour
You are my knight in shining armour.

Your body is gilded and chiselled
And I am bowled over, dazzled
Overpowered by what I see
Swept by beautiful waves of the sea.

Never Forget You

You bade me farewell so I could, never
Forget your love, ever
In my heart, tied a knot
Your eyes saying forget me not.

I will never forget the touch
Of your gentle hands, ouch.
They sear your brand on, so hot
That I shall forget not.

A love that simmers constantly
So as not to boil itself over instantly
Burning with such serenity
From here to infinity.

As you stroked me, my heart burned.
As your farewell, my mind turned
To each other we clung
By love's sting stung.

Your lingering smile
Lasted more than a walk of a mile
The warmth spreading to your face
In the goodbyes of love's race.

I lifted you closer to my chest
Our lips sealed as if to test
Our love and its strength
A breath with no end to its length.

I will forget not
Your eyes peering and hot
I snuggled you as I heard your moans
Despairing at the transience of time, nature loans.

The Simmering

I hate and love the tension
Now that you caught my attention
Yet dare I not mention
Loving you was not my intention.

Yet loving you I did
If I have to be candid
With his arrow cupid
Heated a heart that was tepid.

It was will we, will we not
The love simmering hot
Bubbling in the love pot
We nearly lost the plot.

Your eyes peered into mine
And I heard your heart pine
So my heart was not fine
Yearning with yours to entwine.

We thought we were strong
To resist a love with no wrong
Our sighs grew ever so long
We desired, to each other, to belong.

Even when it was time to part
We kept our hands apart
Fearing the simmering would start
A fire from which we wouldn't depart.

Our love simmered
And our eyes shimmered
With longing our hearts whimpered
At last we hugged, kissed and whispered.

Our Argentine Tango

We hold each other close and
Nose to nose we stand
Our eyes on each other locked
Our hearts in love cloaked.

Will we, will we not?
Flick, flick, sharp and hot
The languid unwinding
Of your leg and the grinding.

Off we race across the floor.
Who is first to open the heart's door?
In and out with hip and foot
Sparks across the floor, we shoot.

Then we pause and
You giro as I stand
Solidly pivot and stay
To feel your sway.

Love's Viennese Waltz

One, two, three. One, two, three
Light on the feet and free
Joined at the hips
Separated at the lips.

Rise and fall, rise and fall
Like the chest wall
Breathing in and out
Like steps with no gout.

Love with an elegance
And delicacy of love's dance
That walks through life
As if on the edge of a knife.

The Rumba of Love

I want to hold you, yet I don't
Caress you, yet I won't
So I keep you at arm's length
Yet we have the same wavelength.

I sinuously keep my arm away
While you turn and sway
And my hips taut but not gaunt
Sway, as yours, my eyes taunt.

I keep my hands off but I'm not irate
As your body and hips gyrate
Sinuously I respond
And our moves correspond.

Our gazes focus and lock
We remain oblivious to the clock
And dare time stand still
As emotions, our hearts, fill.

Then you slither down and hold
My leg like I have told
You this is the end
The music notes, us send.

Then our eyes smoulder
As each arm rotates at the shoulder
And our hearts dance their own rumba
As our love sings its number.

For You I Long

As the beauty of the mountain
View breaks before me
I can't even begin to contain
The depth of the feeling in me

For you, I long
And your beauty, I yearn
To you, I belong
It's a lesson I had to learn.

Life seems to stand still
And the hands of time to go slow
Only empty space to fill
The ebb of a tide so low.

As in your absence
For you I long and sigh
My being and essence
If only you were nigh.

Yet, you are tangible
In my heart, ever present
Pure and incorrigible
Your love to my heart a present.

I feel you in my brain
And with my heart hear
Your thoughts and their train
Though you are not near.

The smile you bring
To my heart is a treasure
More than a diamond ring
Is love without measure?

When I Sit and Listen

The world and around us, everything
Ceases to exist as if nothing
Was created that means something
Except what we share and to us is the thing.

When I sit, listen and see
Your words flowing into the sea
Of my myriad thoughts from A, B to C
I hear the sweetest major chord, C.

I feel contended inside
As I sit by your side
Love that won't subside
Gives me no downside.

It's as if I was born to be there
By your side feels like it's where
Heaven has coded its loveware
And I'm infected everywhere.

It's as if we have known each other
As those who sucked from one mother
Our eyes naturally beckon one another
As our hearts our feelings gather.

When by your side I sit and listen
And our eyes widen and glisten
They talk with languages that soften
The blow of love by which we are smitten.

Puzzle of Love

I hate that I miss you as soon
As you leave, as the light of the moon
Starts to adorn you with its beautiful glow
Like an angel fallen low.

I don't want to fall for your charms
Yet it feels so right, when I am in your arms
I don't feel the urgent fiery passion and fire
Yet your company I continuously desire.

It is the puzzle of love
An ideal so lofty above
That makes us love deeply
As we fall gradually and steeply.

When I first saw you
A face in the crowd were you
Your beauty I noted with my mind
There was no love at first sight, to find.

Then I wonder when no brimstone and fire
Throws us into each other's arms with desire
And we engage in small talk
Like pupils toying aimlessly with chalk.

I tell you it's good to make a fresh start.
You say it will tear you apart
I must keep in touch even as I want
To let go of what I need but can't.

Ache of Love

Loving you is a pain
As sweet as kissing in the rain
Pain so full of happiness
Pounds the heart with no kindness.

The ache of love is like a fire
Burning the heart with desire
Makes the eyes smoulder
When your head is on my shoulder.

Longing for you is the pain of birth
That I will endure for future mirth
What our hearts are creating
Into our souls, is permeating.

I hold you in my arms and desist
In case the earth ceases to exist
If our lips touch and melt
Memories of what we have felt.

My eyes trail into your soul
Wherein there is nothing foul
Just a song my heart finds
As our eyes weld our minds.

Goodbyes are long
Forever we belong
In each other's gaze
Love's ache to faze.

Like the tremolo of a mandolin
And the sustained notes of a violin
The ache of love rises and moans
To a crescendo of sighs and groans.

Oh, You Make Me Happy

When the whole world seems
To be weighing on my shoulders
And everyone deems
The earth in flames, smoulders.

The smile, to my face you bring
Makes my heart well inside
As to a thirsting hart, does a spring
When you stand by my side.

When on your face, my eyes alight
My whole being lights up
I shine from inside out to light
Your world as your heart, I cup.

Oh, you make me ever
Happy I can't stop playing
Love songs and shall never
"I love you", stop saying.

I smile myself to sleep
Thoughts of you a lullaby
Knowing I am in deep
There will be no goodbye.

You Speak My Mind

The words on my lips, you speak
Before I open my mouth
And take me to the peak
Of a journey to the south.

My very breath you exhale
The nectar of your lips I
Get drunk on and tell a tale
Of one by love made high.

I think and before I say it you say
My thoughts out loud
And the ghost in my head lay
On the lightest feathery cloud.

Just as I think what a beautifully spent
Night we have shared so far
You tell me I can stay the night, with intent
And leave the door of your heart ajar.

Before I say that I need
Help, you say if at all
By word or deed need
Help, to give you a call.

I thought you wanted me in your
Arms and you gave me the best
Embrace as your love, you pour
With arms that speak peace and rest.

The Surprise of Love

Love full of surprise
Hits with a hammer blow
Fells one so as never to rise
On love's memorial to lie low.

It grips with a force
Fills with emotion
That shows no remorse
Till one's life is in commotion.

Love full of surprise, creeps
In with surreptitious certainty
No rhyme and reason keeps
It from enduring eternity.

It mellows the hardened
Edges of a life-worn face
Adorns with beauty the softened
Rugged face covered in lace.

Love full of surprise swarms
Hearts with many a pleasant thought
That with craftiness charms
Hearts into a knot to be caught.

Forget You

Even when I want to forget
You, I see you in nothing
And nothing will ever get
Silent. I hear you in everything.

Your beautiful silhouette, shadows cast
And I, a beaten path follow
As my weary feet draw me fast
To your voice that is mellow.

Even the gentle wind whispers
Your name, the waves do the same
Every tongue twists and lispers
And sweetest sounds your name.

I come back to your feet when
I run away, around the world
I can't forget you even then
My thoughts, around you, whirled.

Every song I sing says
Wherever I go I will find
You in many ways
Forever in my mind.

In every story I hear you
With every breath I love
You, every colour your hue
Beautiful like the sky above.

Love Beautifies

The brush of love paints
With best strokes that caress
On canvas to create saints
Perfect and blameless.

Love gives the eyes lenses to part
And refract ugliness into beauty
Makes the dull and stupid smart
From procreation removes the duty.

From love's vantage on its hill top
All the eyes behold is an idyllic view
In which love feasts without a stop
All that matters is your lover and you.

Love gives unique beauty to faults
Makes them special adornments
Which are stored in hearts' vaults
As precious jewels and ornaments.

Belief in a lover's goodness
Denial of all their unkindness
Selective inattention to their rudeness
Keeps love's eyes in blindness.

Love beautifies the plain
With a myriad of the brain's flowers
Takes away the sting of pain
That is love and its infallible powers.

Fragile Love

We embraced each other lightly
Daring not to show too much passion
Guarded and cautious
Yet madly in love.

Like two proud gladiators
Sizing each other up
We took our time to engage
In the titanic battle of love.

We knew it would be bruising
Committing our hearts
To chase our dreams yet
Travel the long journey of love.

Our hands lightly touched
As if our bodies, fragile
To breaking point, would
Shatter under the strain of love.

There was something tender
Soft, in our prolonged goodbye
A farewell embrace, ever so light
We barely touched, afraid of love.

Afraid of the torrent it would release
We looked at each other with
Eyes that implored for more yet
Reined in the rage of love.

The Beat of Our Hearts Next to Each Other

Our eyes met and locked
Hearts lingered and looked
By the power of love shocked
To the core, by love cooked.

Our hearts leapt within
Us, two in a love race
None of us would ev'r win
Racing with the same pace.

The rhythm and beat of our
Hearts to each other in time
Melts away each hour
As hearts next to each other, rhyme.

The hearts beat with a code
Love only gives to the eyes
As if love was of one mode
That gives longing and sighs.

As we cling and embrace
And eyes peer into each other
Under our breasts, hearts come face
To face and dance without bother.

The beat of our hearts starts
A dance to a love song
Fits all the jigsaw parts
Of the love for which we long.

As We Stood on the Deck

Looking over the spreading water
Our minds each other read.
Eyes locked with a gaze that did not falter.
The warmth of love to our hearts spread.

Each of our faces, a smile lit
With longing our eyes moistened.
We drew closer, into each other's arms to fit.
Our voices' caresses softened.

Your shoulder squared to mine.
Our hearts beat in unison.
I was love drunk as if by wine
Struck by Cupid's poison.

We studied the waters below
Shimmering in the sunlight
Quivering hearts made us glow
Stirred by the romance of the sight.

Your eyes smiled into mine.
My heart missed a beat.
My breath rarefied to a mist so fine
Created rainbows from love's feat.

Your beauty I inhaled
Overpowered, I surrendered.
My heart on your spike impaled
Love and life rendered.

Eye to Eye

Eyes tell the story of love
Our hearts with peace to fill
The message of a dove
Strife has ended and we sit still.

Eye to eye
The lock of our gaze
Searching low and high
Through love's maze.

I caress you with my eyes
Gently stroking with invisible hands.
Yours reply with languid sighs.
A soft moan in my ear lands.

You can't bear it anymore
Slide your loins towards mine
Eyes wanting more
Your gaze searching for a sign.

My heart is not ready.
My stillness exasperates
You see I stay steady.
Love never evaporates.

Through the sands of time
Eyes confess I am ever yours.
In my brain you are sublime.
My heart to yours, love pours.

Sing to Me

I hear your heart's melody
To my ear the sweetest sound
Never will my love be a parody
When yours my heart has found.

Sing to me my dearest
I waltz under the mistletoe
To the voice of the fairest
My heart echoes with a falsetto.

In conversation your voice
Mellows with no bellows.
Husky when you know you're my choice
And I'm yours among all fellows.

Romance envelopes me in your musk
I smile from ear to ear
When in your voice, I hear the husk
Sexy is the sound I hear.

Sing to me the tune of love.
Conduct my heart's staves and bars.
Seduce me and coo like a dove.
Produce waves to woo me to the stars.

At night, I hear your husky song
Meanwhile, with a smile I go to sleep
Knowing your song will last long
In the bed of love, in sleep, I'm deep.

Do I Bring Warmth to Your Heart?

You've given me a new understanding
Of love, far above where I knew it to reach
Beyond the heart's pond, it keeps on expanding
Love that impossible walls, will breach.

Now I want to give you
The whole world, in your heart packaged
Wish around the entire universe you flew
Free from the dire verse of a bird that's caged.

Do I bring warmth to your heart when
The wintry world is bitter and cold
Bring a smile with the words I pen
Make you invigorated as you grow old?

Do I stroke away the sadness from the past?
Light your heart with the fire in my eyes?
Whose flame, a lifetime will last
To banish the melancholy sighs

Does the warmth of my love infuse
Throughout your heart and blood stream?
Do you feel the pulse of my love refuse
To stay cold in your unfulfilled dream?

You Know It's Love (When It Shares the Best)

You know it's not love at all
When it's not generous but selfish
Love is not full of gall
With hope it is always bullish.

Love opens the hand to bare all
Above all does not seek
To hold onto one's stall
Nor remain hidden like layers of a leek.

You know it's love when it shares
It's best when it shines
Spares not its wares
Knows no peace when the other pines.

Love does not boast in success
Meekly shares and sows
Making sure it holds no excess
Raising others from their lows.

That's why I give you all I know
Wipe all sadness from your face
My life and heart on you bestow
By my side, give you space.

In the Moonlight

We walked hand in hand
Up and down the undulating land
Unaware of the rising damp
The moonlight to our feet a lamp.

Your face was bright
Reflecting the moonlight
Full of love and joy
Nothing would your heart, annoy.

In the moonlight we stood still
Passion's sighs flowed at will
We peered into each other's eyes
In the valley we were on love's highs.

We clung to each other
Felt the clouds of passion gather
The hands of time stood still
The beat of our hearts the silent night to fill.

Our lips touched and merged
By the fire in us urged
We forgot everything else existed
Only our love subsisted.

We kissed till the early hours of the morning
All cares and worries abandoning
We held each other tight
You were my angel in the moonlight.

You Take My Breath

Each time I look at you
Your beauty I see anew
No part of you is askew
Right through bone and sinew.

You took my breath away
Enthralled by you I stay
In a dreamy meadow I lay
Dazed by your beauty I sway.

I can't help but smile
When I behold you from a mile
Admire your swagger and style
With your gaze, you hold me all the while.

Thoughts of love into my brain stray
"I love you" is all I want to say
For your lasting health I pray
That nothing brings your heart dismay.

You take my breath away as I stew
In the love pot you brew
Each day as my love grew
You were the one, I knew.

I Think of You All the Time

Hardly a moment passes
Without you in my thought
The air whispers your name
The wind carries your love
All of the compasses
Give love the direction sought
The love in my heart a flame.

I think of you all the time
Always, my mind on you dwells
Every time I hear your name
It's like the sweetest sound ever made
Your face and form are sublime
Love inside me swells
Nothing will ever be the same.

Each beautiful thing I see
Reminds me of you, my angel
I am not me without you
It's like your dwelling is inside me
We are matched down to a tee
Our thoughts have mingled and now gel
Fresh like the morning dew.

Goodbye Is Sweet and Sorrowful

The moments we are together
Are the sweetest yet
Our minds are as if on ether
Free from pain and upset.

But we can't always be together forever
Time for parting comes as certain as death
Interferes with our desire and longing to be ever
Entwined in body, soul and mind here on earth.

We amble around and talk
More searching in each other's eyes
We stand still and stop the walk
Sore with desire to say no goodbyes.

The look you give me, my
Love each time we part haunts
Me up to the time in my bed I lie
As your love beckons and taunts.

Parting is sweet
And sorrowful
We say goodbyes as eyes meet
We tarry, though of time, we are mindful.

Because I Loved You

You will never know
For I stooped so low
To set you free from me
When you were on bended knee.

I know it was a low blow
For you will never know
How much I loved you
Even now the pain feels new.

You were the only one
And I wish there was none.
Your kiss made my world
Spin, my heart swelled.

Each hour, our love was our paradise.
We looked forward with each sunrise
To be together daily and I miss
The way you toss your head back when we kiss.

Though, I miss your kiss
It was not remiss
I left you because I loved you.
I carried baggage you knew.

You Gave Me Wings

I was crawling on the ground
In a circle, going round
And round to nowhere fast
Till I met you at last.

You gave me wings
Like a bird my heart sings
Now brave, I reach for the sky
On a wave I breach gravity and fly high.

Now I see a vision
From the vantage of your provision
And see the bigger picture
The horizon is beyond conjecture.

I feel lighter than the air
I soar with a certain flair
An obstacle is like a training aid
To unshackle my potential, as you said.

I enjoy the bird's eye view
From which my past I review
Now free from the nettle's stings
For you gave me wings.

I Thought I Could Forget You

You were manna from heaven
Your love unfermented by leaven
With a heart that was loving
And so caring I felt mine moving.

I thought I could forget you
But like honey dew
The taste of your lips I
Remember its sweetness: sigh.

How can I forget ever
Sitting on the bench with the fever
Of love driving us crazy
Clouding our vision hazy.

Around us were flowers and all greens
We felt like we were back in our teens
Fresh and free from any stench
As we made out on the bench.

I slowly put a grape onto your mouth
You slowly put a grape in my mouth
We took turns to bite chocolate pieces
And shared the sweetest kisses.

You were one special romantic soul
Passionate, with nothing foul
I well up when I think of us
Listening to Dolly Parton in that bus.

When You Meet
Someone Special

A fire is lit inside you
To give you a youthful glow
With sudden energy that's new
Your steps are no longer slow
You feel on top of a mountain
Rise up to the celestial
You drink from a fresh fountain
When you meet someone special.

You get in touch with your feelings
With who you are. Content.
Certain in your dealings
You maintain focus on your intent
Dreams of the impossible
Your daily bread
The ordinary no longer admissible
Your wings you spread.

You stop looking for happiness outside
Of yourself but spread it
From deep inside
Your joy is lit
Your smile becomes infectious
You have found a diamond
You have tasted the delicious
Chocolate with your favourite almond.

Something Always Lingers

Between us
Something always lingers
Rich like humus
Tarrying in our trailing fingers.

We say goodbye
Stay standing next to each other
Our connection refusing to die
Glances go from one to another.

You look at me as if you want
From me some special words
I am not sure, yet so I can't
We linger closer like lovebirds.

Your gaze holds mine
And asks a question
My mouth does not feel fine
Holds onto the words I can't mention.

We embrace with tenderness
Longing eyes peer into each other
Fearing to part towards loneliness
We cling, one to another.

Love at First Sight (I Wish)

It would have helped a lot
Falling in love at first sight
Unfortunately, I was not
Just left you unfulfilled that night.

I tried so hard not to fall
In love, I knew you were
Into my court you threw the ball
To catch, I was not yet there.

Stranger than fiction
My heart began to melt
To you like an addiction
Increasingly, love was all I felt.

By the time I felt what your heart had
Yours I had worn
My slow warmth had driven you mad
Your heart was already torn.

I wish it had been love at first sight
You were a perfect soulmate
It always feels right
When together but now it's too late.

Blue

Our love is fluid flowing
Between our favourite water colours
Shimmering and glowing
Reflecting us like mirrors.

We never see blue
Together our heads stay above the clouds
Our hearts stay true
Love our thoughts enshrouds.

I smile when I see you wearing blue
The colour that signals depth
I am enshrouded in the same hue
We are on the same wavelength.

Blue is the colour of limitlessness
Going beyond the horizon and the sky
Our love and thoughts are relentless
Together we fly high.

You look handsome in blue
I look pretty in your blue eyes
It's like you knew
The colour blue deepens our ties.

CPSIA information can be obtained
at www.ICGtesting.com
Printed in the USA
BVHW041543230819
556561BV00043B/3504/P